Karmic Visions

By
Helena P. Blavatsky

Copyright © 2022 Lamp of Trismegistus. All rights reserved. No part of this publication may be reproduced or transmitted in any form or by any means, electronic or mechanical, including photocopying, recording, or by any information storage and retrieval system, without permission in writing from Lamp of Trismegistus. Reviewers may quote brief passages.

ISBN: 978-1-63118-621-9

Esoteric Classics

Other Books in this Series and Related Titles

Aurora of the Philosophers by Paracelsus (978-1-63118-507-6)

Rosicrucian Rules, Secret Signs, Codes and Symbols by various (978-1-63118-488-8)

On the Philadelphian Gold by Philochrysus & Philadelphus (978-1-63118-511-3)

Paracelsus, the Four Elements and Their Spirits by M P Hall (978-1-63118-400-0)

The Stone of the Philosophers by A E Waite (978-1-63118-509-0)

Clairvoyance and Psychic Abilities by A Besant &c (978-1-63118-403-1)

The Rosicrucian Chemical Marriage by Christian Rosenkreuz (978-1-63118-458-1)

The Alchemical Catechism of Paracelsus by Paracelsus (978-1-63118-513-7)

Alchemy in the Nineteenth Century by Helena P. Blavatsky (978-1-63118-446-8)

Rosicrucians and Speculative Masonry in the Seventeenth Century (978-1-63118-489-5)

Qabbalistic Teachings and the Tree of Life by M P Hall (978-1-63118-482-6)

The Sepher Yetzirah and the Qabalah by M P Hall (978-1-63118-481-9)

The Devil in Love by Jacques Cazotte (978–1–63118–499–4)

Fortune-Telling with Dice by Astra Cielo (978-1-63118-466-6)

History, Analysis and Secret Tradition of the Tarot by Hall &c (978-1-63118-445-1)

Crystal Vision Through Crystal Gazing by Frater Achad (978-1-63118-455-0)

The Golden Verses of Pythagoras: Five Translations (978-1-63118-479-6)

Arcane Formulas or Mental Alchemy by W W Atkinson (978-1-63118-459-8)

The Machinery of the Mind by Dion Fortune (978-1-63118-451-2)

The A E Waite Reader: A Selection of Occult Essays (978-1-63118-515-1)

The Leadbeater Reader: A Selection of Occult Essays (978-1-63118-483-3)

Audio versions are also available on Audible, Amazon and Apple

Other Books in this Series and Related Titles

The Ascension of Isaiah by Isaiah (978-1-63118-620-2)

The Mysteries of Mithra by G R S Mead (978-1-63118-619-6)

Second Book of Enoch by Enoch (978-1-63118-617-2)

Lost Keys of Freemasonry by Manly P Hall (978-1-63118-616-5)

Book of the Watchers by Enoch (978-1-63118-615-8)

Sepher Yetzirah and the Qabalah by Manly P Hall (978-1-63118-614-1)

Philosophy of Self-Knowledge by Franz Hartmann (978-1-63118-613-4)

Occult Symbolism of the Sun and Moon, the Goddess Isis and thee Solar Deities by Manly P Hall (978–1–63118–611–0)

Practical Theosophy by Annie Besant (978–1–63118–610–3)

The Human Body in Symbolism by Manly P Hall (978–1–63118–609–7)

Theosophical Basics by William Q Judge (978–1–63118–608–0)

The Hebrew Talisman by Richard Harte (978–1–63118–607–3)

Early Masonic Symbolism by Manly P Hall (978–1–63118–606–6)

Nature Spirits and Elementals by Louise Off (978-1-63118-605-9)

Swedenborg Bifrons by H P Blavatsky (978-1-63118-604-2)

Practical Use of Psychic Powers by C W Leadbeater (978-1-63118-603-5)

Using White & Black Magic by C W Leadbeater (978-1-63118-602-8)

Jesus, the Last Great Initiate by Edouard Schure (978-1-63118-599-1)

Mysterious Wonders of Antiquity by Manly P Hall (978-1-63118-598-4)

Ancient Mysteries and Secret Societies by Manly P Hall (978–1–63118–597–7)

The Zodiac and Its Signs by Manly P Hall (978–1–63118–596–0)

Audio versions are also available on Audible, Amazon and Apple

Table of Contents

Introduction...7

Karmic Visions

Forward...9

I...13

II...17

III...19

IV...21

V...23

VI...27

VII...29

VIII...31

IX...35

X...37

XI...41

INTRODUCTION

The word "esoteric" can be difficult to define. Esotericism in general can be seen less as a system of beliefs and more as a category, which encompasses numerous, different systems of beliefs. It's a bit of juxtaposition, since the word "esoteric" indicates something that few people know about, while the term itself broadly covers numerous philosophies, practices, areas of study and belief systems.

In a greater sense, Esotericism acts as a storehouse for secret knowledge, which is often considered ancient (by *tradition, if not by fact*), passed down from generation to generation, in private. At various times in history, simply possessing the knowledge of some of these subjects, was considered illegal and a jailable offence, if discovered. This usually included such general topics as Alchemy, Pharmacology, Qabalah, Hermeticism, Occultism, Ceremonial Magic, Astrology, Divination, Rosicrucianism and so on. Collectively, these areas of study were often referred to as the esoteric sciences.

Sometimes, the outer garment of a subject isn't esoteric, while what is hidden beneath it, is. As an example, Freemasonry isn't necessarily esoteric by nature (at *least not anymore*), but certain signs, passwords and handshakes given to the candidate during their initiation, are in fact, esoteric, in the sense that they are hidden from the general public.

Today, in the twenty-first century, such topics are readily available at bookstores across the country, and numerous main-steam publishers offer beginners guides and coffee-table volumes on many of these subjects, intended for mass appeal. Books like *"The Secret"* have turned previously arcane topics into household knowledge. All that being the case, however, it isn't to say that there still aren't buried secrets to uncover, ancient wisdom being ignored and forgotten mysteries to be explored. In fact, it is often that we are only able to further our own studies by standing on the shoulders of these disappearing giants.

Lamp of Trismegistus is doing its part to help preserve humanity's esoteric history by making some of these classics available to those students who are seeking to unearth the knowledge of these ancient colossi.

So, be sure to check other titles from our *Esoteric Classics* series, as well as our *Occult Fiction*, *Theosophical Classics*, *Foundations of Freemasonry Series*, *Supernatural Fiction*, *Paranormal Research Series*, *Studies in Buddhism* and our *Christian Apocrypha Series*. You can also download the audio versions of most of these titles from Amazon, Apple or Audible, for learning on the go.

FOREWORD

This Prophetic study of the workings of the Law of Karma (Cause and Effect) in European history from the fifth century onwards, was written twenty-six years before the Great War began in 1914. It is reprinted in this series because on page 6 of No.7, "H. P. Blavatsky on Dreams" she says: "Our 'dreams', being simply the waking state and actions of the true Self, must be, of course, recorded somewhere. Read 'Karmic Visions' in Lucifer, and note the description of the real Ego, sitting as a spectator of the life of the hero, and perhaps something will strike you". From Section 2 onwards a very clear distinction is drawn between the "Soul-Ego" and the "Form" in which it is re-born.

Written by one who had been trained and initiated in the Oriental science of Yoga Vidya, which pierces the veil of Illusion and reveals the inner workings of Karma, this study of the conversion of a "Soul-Ego" by experience and suffering from War to Peace, must surely be of greatly increased interest and importance since the tremendous lessons of 1914-18. The information given in the footnotes is added in order to assist the reader to understand what is here taught by a great historical illustration. "Karmic Visions" was published shortly after the death of the Emperor Frederick in June, 1888. In the previous January number of Lucifer, H.P.B. had written in her New Year editorial: "It is not likely that much happiness or prosperity can come to those who are living for the truth under such a dark number as 1888; but still the year is heralded by the glorious star Venus-Lucifer, shining so resplendently that is has been mistaken for that still rarer visitor, the star of Bethlehem. This too, is at hand; and surely something of the Christos spirit must be born upon earth under such conditions". Again, in the January number, 1889, she wrote: "A year ago it was stated that 1888 was a dark combination of numbers; it has proved so since ..... Almost every nation was visited by some dire calamity. Prominent among other countries was Germany. It was in 1888 that the Empire reached, virtually, the 18th year of its unification. It was during the fatal combination of the four numbers 8 that it lost two of its Emperors, and planted the seeds of many dire Karmic results".

That in writing with such prophetic insight H. P. Blavatsky was quite impersonal, is clear from her other writings of a similar character. Moreover, she was herself German on her father's side (Mecklenberg Counts von Hahn) her mother being a daughter of Princess Dolgorouki. For what she wrote concerning the French Revolution as the result of the "selfish tyranny of the French kings", and her own military service under Garibaldi against the Papal power, see Buddhism the Science of Life, 22nd. ed. pp. 110-115.

Oh, sad no more! Oh, sweet No more!
Oh, strange No more!
By a mossed brook bank on a stone
I smelt a wild weed-flower alone;
There was a ringing in my ears,
And both my eyes gushed out with tears,
Surely all pleasant things had gone before,
Low buried fathom deep beneath with three, NO MORE.

— Tennyson ["*The Gem*" 1831]

I

A camp filled with war-chariots, neighing horses and legions of long-haired soldiers . . .

A regal tent, gaudy in its barbaric splendour. Its linen walls are weighed down under the burden of arms. In its centre a raised seat covered with skins, and on it a stalwart, savage-looking warrior. He passes in review prisoners of war brought in turn before him, who are disposed of according to the whim of the heartless despot.

A new captive is now before him, and is addressing him with passionate earnestness . . . As he listens to her with suppressed passion in his manly, but fierce, cruel face, the balls of his eyes become bloodshot and roll with fury. And as he bends forward with fierce stare, his whole appearance — his matted locks hanging over the frowning brow, his big-boned body with strong sinews, and the two large hands resting on the shield placed upon the right knee — justifies the remark made in hardly audible whisper by a grey-headed soldier to his neighbour:

"Little mercy shall the holy prophetess receive at the hands of Clovis!"

The captive, who stands between two Burgundian warriors, facing the ex-prince of the Salians, now king of all the Franks, is an old woman with silver-white dishevelled hair, hanging over her skeleton-like shoulders. In spite of her great age, her tall figure is erect; and the inspired black eyes look proudly and fearlessly into the cruel face of the treacherous son of Gilderich. [*Clovis 1 (470-511), or Hlodowing, only son of Gilderich or Hilderic, Chief of the Salian Franks, who died in 481. In 486 he swept away the only Roman power left in*

Northern Gaul and made Paris his capital, establishing the dynasty of the Merovingian kings. He married Clothilde, niece of the Burgundian king, and became a Christian under her influence after repelling the invasion of the Allemanni in 496. In this alliance the Church became more warlike, the Frank more civilised. The Burgundians were reduced in 500, the Visigoths of the Rhone Valley under Alaric in 507, thus bringing practically the whole of modern France into the Frankish kingdom, the first to arise out of the wreck of the Roman Empire. For 150 years the Frankish kingdom was split into Neustria (speaking a Latinish tongue) and Austrasia, the Rhineland which remained German. Reunited in the eight century under Charlemagne, it held together until the death of his grandson in 840, when the final division took place. "The grim Frank" (Clovis 1,) says the writer in the Encyc. Brit., "vigorous and ambitious, knew neither scruple nor pity, and the clergy round his throne passed over crimes which they were powerless to prevent ..... From him modern France rightly dates her beginning ..... For five centuries after his death in 511 the history of France must be regarded as subordinate to that of Germany." Editor.]

"Aye, King," she says, in a loud, ringing voice. "Aye, thou art great and mighty now, but thy days are numbered, and thou shalt reign but three summers longer. Wicked thou wert born . . . perfidious thou art to thy friends and allies, robbing more than one of his lawful crown. Murderer of thy next-of-kin, thou who addest to the knife and spear in open warfare, dagger, poison and treason, beware how thou dearest with the servant of Nerthus!" [*"The Nourishing" (Tacit. Germ. XI) — the Earth, a Mother-Goddess, the most beneficent deity of the ancient Germans.*]

"Ha, ha, ha! . . . old hag of Hell!" chuckles the King, with an evil, ominous sneer. "Thou hast crawled out of the entrails of thy mother-goddess truly. Thou fearest not my wrath? It is well. But little need I fear thine empty imprecations . . . I, a baptized Christian!"

"So, so," replies the Sybil. "All know that Clovis has abandoned the gods of his fathers; that he has lost all faith in the warning voice of the white horse of the Sun, and that out of fear of the Allimani he went serving on his knees Remigius, the servant of the Nazarene, at Rheims. But hast thou become any truer in thy new faith? Hast thou not murdered in cold blood all thy brethren who trusted in thee, after, as well as before, thy apostasy? Hast not thou plighted troth to Alaric, the King of the West Goths, and hast thou not killed him by stealth, running thy spear into his back while he was bravely fighting an enemy? And is it thy new faith and thy new gods that teach thee to be devising in thy black soul even now foul means against Theodoric, who put thee down? . . . Beware, Clovis, beware! For now the gods of thy fathers have risen against thee! Beware, I say, for . . . "

"Woman!" fiercely cries the King — "Woman, cease thy insane talk and answer my question. Where is the treasure of the grove amassed by thy priests of Satan, and hidden after they had been driven away by the Holy Cross? . . . Thou alone knowest. Answer, or by Heaven and Hell I shall thrust thy evil tongue down thy throat for ever!" . . .

She heeds not the threat, but goes on calmly and fearlessly as before, as if she had not heard.

".....The gods say, Clovis, thou art accursed..... Clovis, thou shalt be reborn among thy present enemies, and suffer the tortures thou hast inflicted upon thy victims. All the combined power and glory thou hast deprived them of shall be thine in prospect, yet thou shalt never reach it! . . . Thou shalt . . . "

The prophetess never finishes her sentence.

With a terrible oath the King, crouching like a wild beast on his skin-covered seat, pounces upon her with the leap of a jaguar, and with one blow fells her to the ground. And as he lifts his sharp murderous spear the "Holy One" of the Sun-worshipping tribe makes the air ring with a last imprecation.

"I curse thee, enemy of Nerthus! May my agony be tenfold thine! . . . May the Great Law avenge. . . .

The heavy spear falls, and, running through the victim's throat, nails the head to the ground. A stream of hot crimson blood gushes from the gaping wound and covers king and soldiers with indelible gore . . .

II

Time — the landmark of gods and men in the boundless field of Eternity, the murderer of its offspring and of memory in mankind — time moves on with noiseless, incessant step through aeons and ages . . . Among millions of other Souls, a Soul-Ego is reborn: for weal or for woe, who knoweth! Captive in its new human Form, it grows with it, and together they become, at last, conscious of their existence. [*This term "Soul-Ego" should not be mistaken for what, in certain post. H.P.B. speculations, is called "the growing soul"(a term never used by her), as it clearly refers to the Ego, the "Spectator", which she calls "the real Ego..... the Higher Ego" whose "thoughts and Voice" are "Voice of his Conscience" for the "temporary and evanescent personality" here called the "Form." See "H. P. Blavatsky on Dreams" page 3. Editor*]

Happy are the years of their blooming youth, unclouded with want or sorrow. Neither knows aught of the Past nor of the Future. For them all is the joyful Present: for the Soul-Ego is unaware that it had ever lived in other human tabernacles, it knows not that it shall be again reborn, and it takes no thought of the morrow.

Its Form is calm and content. It has hitherto given its Soul-Ego no heavy troubles. Its happiness is due to the continuous mild serenity of its temper, to the affection it spreads wherever it goes. For it is a noble Form, and its heart is full of benevolence. Never has the Form startled its Soul-Ego with a too-violent shock, or otherwise disturbed the calm placidity of its tenant.

Two score of years glide by like one short pilgrimage; a long walk through the sun-lit paths of life, hedged by ever-blooming roses with no thorns. The rare sorrows that befall the twin pair, Form and Soul, appear to them rather like the pale light of the cold northern moon, whose beams throw into a deeper shadow all around the moon-lit objects, than as the blackness of the night, the night of hopeless sorrow and despair.

Son of a Prince, born to rule himself one day his father's kingdom; surrounded from his cradle by reverence and honours; deserving of the universal respect and sure of the love of all — what could the Soul-Ego desire more for the Form it dwelt in.

And so the Soul-Ego goes on enjoying existence in its tower of strength, gazing quietly at the panorama of life ever changing before its two windows — the two kind blue eyes of a loving and good man. [*Frederick III of Russia (1831-1888). Under the influence chiefly of his father in-law, the English Prince Consort, he became a strong Liberal differing widely from the policy of Bismarck. Privately he was opposed to the war of 1866 with Austria in Holstein, although it was the timely arrival of his army which won the decisive battle of Königgrätz on July 3rd. In the Franco-German War of 1870 he again led his army at Wörth and Sedan, and took part in the siege of Paris. When the Coalition of Liberal Parties was formed in 1884 it was popularly known as "the Crown Prince's Party", although he carefully refrained from doing anything to embarrass his father's government. He was the great hope of the Liberals on his succession to the throne in March 1888, but unfortunately for the peace of Europe he died of cancer of the throat in the following June. — Editor*]

III

One day an arrogant and boisterous enemy threatens the father's kingdom, and the savage instincts of the warrior of old awaken in the Soul-Ego. It leaves its dreamland amid the blossoms of life and causes its Ego of clay to draw the soldier's blade, assuring him it is in defence of his country.

Prompting each other to action, they defeat the enemy and cover themselves with glory and pride. They make the haughty foe bite the dust at their feet in supreme humiliation. For this they are crowned by history with the unfading laurels of valour, which are those of success. They make a footstool of the fallen enemy and transform their sire's little kingdom into a great empire. Satisfied they could achieve no more for the present, they return to seclusion and to the dreamland of their sweet home.

For three lustra more the Soul-Ego sits at its usual post, beaming out of its windows on the world around. Over its head the sky is blue and the vast horizons are covered with those seemingly unfading flowers that grow in the sunlight of health and strength. All looks fair as a verdant mead in spring . . .

IV

But an evil day comes to all in the drama of being. It waits through the life of king and of beggar. It leaves traces on the history of every mortal born from woman, and it can neither be seared away, entreated, nor propitiated. Health is a dewdrop that falls from the heavens to vivify the blossoms on earth, only during the morn' of life, its spring and summer . . . It has but a short duration and returns from whence it came — the invisible realms.

> How oft'neath the bud that is brightest and fairest,
> The seeds of the canker in embryo lurk!
> How oft at the root of the flower that is rarest —
> Secure in its ambush the worm is at work. . . . . ."

The running sand which moves downward in the glass, wherein the hours of human life are numbered, runs swifter. The worm has gnawed the blossom of health through its heart. The strong body is found stretched one day on the thorny bed of pain. [*The Crown Prince Frederick was attacked by cancer of the throat in 1887, and spent the following winter at San Remo, undergoing the operation of tracheotomy in January 1888. On March 8th he had to return to Berlin to succeed his father, but reigned only 99 days. See The Fatal Illness of Frederick the Noble, 1888, by Sir Morell Mackenzie, the English throat specialist who attended him. — Editor*]

The Soul-Ego beams no longer. It sits still and looks sadly out of what has become its dungeon windows, on the world which is now rapidly being shrouded for it in the funeral palls of suffering. Is it the eve of night eternal which is nearing?

V

Beautiful are the resorts on the midland sea. An endless line of surf-beaten, black, rugged rocks stretches, hemmed in between the golden sands of the coast and the deep blue waters of the gulf. They offer their granite breast to the fierce blows of the north-west wind and thus protect the dwellings of the rich that nestle at their foot on the inland side. The half-ruined cottages on the open shore are the insufficient shelter of the poor. Their squalid bodies are often crushed under the walls torn and washed down by wind and angry wave. But they only follow the great law of the survival of the fittest. Why should they be protected?

Lovely is the morning when the sun dawns with golden amber tints and its first rays kiss the cliffs of the beautiful shore. Glad is the song of the lark, as, emerging from its warm nest of herbs, it drinks the morning dew from the deep flower-cups; when the tip of the rosebud thrills under the caress of the first sunbeam, and earth and heaven smile in mutual greeting. Sad is the Soul-Ego alone as it gazes on awakening nature from the high couch opposite the large bay-window.

How calm is the approaching noon as the shadow creeps steadily on the sundial towards the hour of rest! Now the hot sun begins to melt the clouds in the limpid air and the last shreds of the morning mist that lingers on the tops of the distant hills vanish in it. All nature is prepared to rest at the hot and lazy hour of midday. The feathered tribes cease their song; their soft, gaudy wings droop and they hang their drowsy heads, seeking refuge from the burning heat. A morning lark is busy nestling in the bordering bushes under the clustering flowers of the pomegranate and the sweet bay of the Mediterranean. The active songster has become voiceless.

"Its voice will resound as joyfully again tomorrow!" sighs the Soul-Ego, as it listens to the dying buzzing of the insects on the verdant turf. "Shall ever mine?"

And now the flower-scented breeze hardly stirs the languid heads of the luxuriant plants. A solitary palm-tree, growing out of the cleft of a moss-covered rock, next catches the eye of the Soul-Ego. Its once upright, cylindrical trunk has been twisted out of shape and half-broken by the nightly blasts of the north-west winds. And as it stretches wearily its drooping feathery arms, swayed to and fro in the blue pellucid air, its body trembles and threatens to break in two at the first new gust that may arise.

"And then, the severed part will fall into the sea, and the once stately palm will be no more," soliloquizes the Soul-Ego as it gazes sadly out of its windows.

Everything returns to life, in the cool, old bower at the hour of sunset. The shadows on the sun-dial become with every moment thicker, and animate nature awakens busier than ever in the cooler hours of approaching night. Birds and insects chirrup and buzz their last evening hymns around the tall and still powerful Form, as it paces slowly and wearily along the gravel walk. And now its heavy gaze falls wistfully on the azure bosom of the tranquil sea. The gulf sparkles like a gem-studded carpet of blue-velvet in the farewell dancing sunbeams, and smiles like a thoughtless, drowsy child, weary of tossing about. Further on, calm and serene in its perfidious beauty, the open sea stretches far and wide the smooth mirror of its cool waters— salt and bitter as human tears. It lies in its treacherous repose like a gorgeous, sleeping monster, watching over the unfathomed mystery of its dark abysses. Truly the monumentless cemetery of the millions sunk in its depths . . .

> "Without a grave,
> Unknell'd, uncoffined and unknown . . . ."

while the sorry relic of the once noble Form pacing yonder, once that its hour strikes and the deep-voiced bells toll the knell for the departed soul, shall be laid out in state and pomp. Its dissolution will be announced by millions of trumpet voices. Kings, princes and the mighty ones of the earth will be present at its obsequies, or will send their representatives with sorrowful faces and condoling messages to those left behind . . .

"One point gained, over those 'uncoffined and unknown'," is the bitter reflection of the Soul-Ego.

Thus glides past one day after the other; and as swift-winged Time urges his flight, every vanishing hour destroying some thread in the tissue of life, the Soul-Ego is gradually transformed in its views of things and men. Flitting between two eternities, far away from its birthplace, solitary among its crowd of physicians, and attendants, the Form is drawn with every day nearer to its Spirit-Soul. Another light unapproached and unapproachable in days of joy, softly descends upon the weary prisoner. It sees now that which it had never perceived before. . . .

VI

How grand, how mysterious are the spring nights on the seashore when the winds are chained and the elements lulled! A solemn silence reigns in nature. Alone the silvery, scarcely audible ripple of the wave, as it runs caressingly over the moist sand, kissing shells and pebbles on its up and down journey, reaches the ear like the regular soft breathing of a sleeping bosom. How small, how insignificant and helpless feels man, during these quiet hours, as he stands between the two gigantic magnitudes, the star-hung dome above, and the slumbering earth below. Heaven and earth are plunged in sleep, but their souls are awake, and they confabulate, whispering one to the other mysteries unspeakable. It is then that the occult side of Nature lifts her dark veils for us, and reveals secrets we would vainly seek to extort from her during the day. The firmament, so distant, so far away from earth, now seems to approach and bend over her. The sidereal meadows exchange embraces with their more humble sisters of the earth — the daisy-decked valleys and the green slumbering fields. The heavenly dome falls prostrate into the arms of the great quiet sea; and the millions of stars that stud the former peep into and bathe in every lakelet and pool. To the grief-furrowed soul those twinkling orbs are the eyes of angels. They look down with ineffable pity on the suffering of mankind. It is not the night dew that falls on the sleeping flowers, but sympathetic tears that drop from those orbs, at the sight of the GREAT HUMAN SORROW . . .

Yes; sweet and beautiful is a southern night. But —

"When silently we watch the bed, by the taper's flickering light,
When all we love is fading fast — how terrible is night. . . ."

VII

Another day is added to the series of buried days. The far green hills, and the fragrant boughs of the pomegranate blossom have melted in the mellow shadows of the night, and both sorrow and joy are plunged in the lethargy of soul-resting sleep. Every noise has died out in the royal gardens, and no voice or sound is heard in that overpowering stillness.

Swift-winged dreams descend from the laughing stars in motley crowds, and landing upon the earth disperse among mortals and immortals, amid animals and men. They hover over the sleepers, each attracted by its affinity and kind; dreams of joy and hope, balmy and innocent visions, terrible and awesome sights seen with sealed eyes, sensed by the soul; some instilling happiness and consolation, others causing sobs to heave the sleeping bosoms, tears and mental torture, all and one preparing unconsciously to the sleepers their waking thoughts of the morrow.

Even in sleep the Soul-Ego finds no rest.

Hot and feverish its body tosses about in restless agony. For it, the time of happy dreams is now a vanished shadow, a long bygone recollection. Through the mental agony of the soul, there lies a transformed man. Through the physical agony of the frame, there flutters in it a fully awakened Soul. The veil of illusion has fallen off from the cold idols of the world, and the vanities and emptiness of fame and wealth stand bare, often hideous, before its eyes. The thoughts of the Soul fall like dark shadows on the cogitative faculties of the fast disorganizing body, haunting the thinker daily, nightly, hourly ... [*The effect of physical and mental suffering in the training and education of the Soul-Ego is strongly emphasised in the*

Esoteric Philosophy and indeed in all Oriental teaching. H. P. Blavatsky once said to her pupils, "Rude physical health is a bar to seership". — Editor]

The sight of his snorting steed pleases him no longer. The recollections of guns and banners wrested from the enemy; of cities razed, of trenches, cannons and tents, of an array of conquered spoils now stirs but little his national pride. Such thoughts move him no more, and ambition has become powerless to awaken in his aching heart the haughty recognition of any valorous deed of chivalry. Visions of another kind now haunt his weary days and long sleepless nights . . .

What he now sees is a throng of bayonets clashing against each other in a mist of smoke and blood; thousands of mangled corpses covering the ground, torn and cut to shreds by the murderous weapons devised by science and civilization, blessed to success by the servants of his God. What he now dreams of are bleeding, wounded and dying men, with missing limbs and matted locks, wet and soaked through with gore . . .

VIII

A hideous dream detaches itself from a group of passing visions, and alights heavily on his aching chest. The nightmare shows him, men expiring on the battlefield with a curse on those who led them to their destruction. Every pang in his own wasting body brings to him in dream the recollection of pangs still worse, of pangs suffered through and for him. He sees and feels the torture of the fallen millions, who die after long hours of terrible mental and physical agony; who expire in forest and plain, in stagnant ditches by the road-side, in pools of blood under a sky made black with smoke. His eyes are once more rivetted to the torrents of blood, every drop of which represents a tear of despair, a heart-rent cry, a lifelong sorrow. He hears again the thrilling sighs of desolation, and the shrill cries ringing through mount, forest and valley. He sees the old mothers who have lost the light of their souls; families, the hand that fed them. He beholds widowed young wives thrown on the wide, cold world, and beggared orphans wailing in the streets by the thousands. He finds the young daughters of his bravest old soldiers exchanging their mourning garments for the gaudy frippery of prostitution, and the Soul-Ego shudders in the sleeping Form... His heart is rent by the groans of the famished; his eyes blinded by the smoke of burning hamlets, of homes destroyed, of towns and cities in smouldering ruins. . . .

And in his terrible dream, he remembers that moment of insanity in his soldier's life, when standing over a heap of the dead and the dying, waving in his right hand a naked sword red to its hilt with smoking blood, and in his left, the colours rent from the hand of the warrior expiring at his feet, he had sent in a stentorian voice praises to the throne of the Almighty, thanksgiving for the victory just obtained! . . .

He starts in his sleep and awakes in horror. A great shudder shakes his frame like an aspen leaf, and sinking back on his pillows, sick at the recollection, he hears a voice — the voice of the Soul-Ego — saying in him:

"Fame and victory are vainglorious words ... Thanksgiving and prayers for lives destroyed — wicked lies and blasphemy!" ...

"What have they brought thee or to thy fatherland, those bloody victories!" ... whispers the Soul in him. "A population clad in iron armour," it replies. "Two score millions of men dead now to all spiritual aspiration and Soul-life. A people, henceforth deaf to the peaceful voice of the honest citizen's duty, averse to a life of peace, blind to the arts and literature, indifferent to all but lucre and ambition. What is thy future Kingdom, now? A legion of war-puppets as units, a great wild beast in their collectivity. A beast that, like the sea yonder, slumbers gloomily now, but to fall with the more fury on the first enemy that is indicated to it. Indicated, by whom? It is as though a heartless, proud Fiend, assuming sudden authority, incarnate Ambition and Power, had clutched with iron hand the minds of a whole country. By what wicked enchantment has he brought the people back to those primeval days of the nation when their ancestors, the yellow-haired Suevi, and the treacherous Franks roamed about in their warlike spirit, thirsting to kill, to decimate and subject each other. By what infernal powers has this been accomplished? Yet the transformation has been produced and it is as undeniable as the fact that alone the Fiend rejoices and boasts of the transformation effected. The whole world is hushed in breathless expectation. Not a wife or mother, but is haunted in her dreams by the black and ominous storm-cloud that overhangs the whole of Europe. The cloud is approaching .... It comes nearer and nearer. ... Oh woe and horror! .... I foresee once more for earth the suffering I have already witnessed. I read the fatal destiny upon the brow of the flower of Europe's youth! [*Prevision of the Great War 1914-18. Editor*] But if I live and have the power, never, oh never shall my country take part in it again! No, no, I will not see —

'The glutton death gorged with devouring lives. . . .'

"I will not hear —

'robb'd mother's shrieks
While from men's piteous wounds and horrid gashes
The lab'ring life flows faster than the blood!' . . . ."

IX

Firmer and firmer grows in the Soul-Ego the feeling of intense hatred for the terrible butchery called war; deeper and deeper does it impress its thoughts upon the Form that holds it captive. Hope awakens at times in the aching breast and colours the long hours of solitude and meditation; like the morning ray that dispels the dusky shades of shadowy despondency, it lightens the long hours of lonely thought. But as the rainbow is not always the dispeller of the storm-clouds but often only a refraction of the setting sun on a passing cloud, so the moments of dreamy hope are generally followed by hours of still blacker despair. Why, oh why, thou mocking Nemesis, hast thou thus purified and enlightened, among all the sovereigns on this earth, him, whom thou hast made helpless, speechless and powerless? Why hast thou kindled the flame of holy brotherly love for man in the breast of one whose heart already feels the approach of the icy hand of death and decay, whose strength is steadily deserting him and whose very life is melting away like foam on the crest of a breaking wave? [*The Karma of the Soul-Ego in its former incarnation as Clovis has not only exacted physical retribution for the slayings of the prophetess, but has also rendered its present personality Frederick powerless to avert the World War of 1914 -18 now so clearly revealed in this vision, in which his son William II was destined to play so fat a part. — Editor*]

And now the hand of Fate is upon the couch of pain. The hour for the fulfilment of nature's law has struck at last. The old Sire is no more; the younger man is henceforth a monarch. Voiceless and helpless, he is nevertheless a potentate, the autocratic master of millions of subjects. Cruel Fate has erected a throne for him over an open grave, and beckons him to glory and to power. Devoured by suffering, he finds himself suddenly crowned. The wasted Form is snatched from its warm nest amid the palm groves and the roses; it is whirled from balmy south to the frozen north, where waters harden into crystal groves and "waves on waves in solid mountains rise"; whither he now speeds to reign and — speeds to die.

X

Onward, onward rushes the black, fire-vomiting monster, devised by man to partially conquer Space and Time. Onward, and further with every moment from the health-giving, balmy South flies the train. Like the Dragon of the Fiery Head, it devours distance and leaves behind it a long trail of smoke, sparks and stench. And as its long, tortuous, flexible body, wriggling and hissing like a gigantic dark reptile, glides swiftly, crossing mountain and moor, forest, tunnel and plain, its swinging monotonous motion lulls the worn-out occupant, the weary and heartsore Form, to sleep . . .

In the moving palace the air is warm and balmy. The luxurious vehicle is full of exotic plants; and from a large cluster of sweet-smelling flowers arises together with its scent the fairy Queen of dreams, followed by her band of joyous elves. The Dryads laugh in their leafy bowers as the train glides by, and send floating upon the breeze dreams of green solitudes and fairy visions. The rumbling noise of wheels is gradually transformed into the roar of a distant waterfall, to subside into the silvery trills of a crystalline brook. The Soul-Ego takes its flight into Dreamland. . . .

It travels through aeons of time, and lives, and feels, and breathes under the most contrasted forms and personages. It is now a giant, a Yotun, who rushes into Muspelheim, where Surtur rules with his flaming sword.

It battles fearlessly against a host of monstrous animals, and puts them to fight with a single wave of its mighty hand. Then it sees itself in the Northern Mistworld, it penetrates under the guise of a brave bowman into Helheim, the Kingdom of the Dead, where a Black-Elf reveals to him a series of its lives and their mysterious concatenation. "Why does man suffer?" enquires the Soul-Ego. "Because he would become one", is the mocking answer. Forthwith, the Soul-Ego stands in the presence of the holy goddess, Saga. She sings to it of the valorous deeds of the Germanic heroes, of their virtues and their vices. She shows the Soul the mighty warriors fallen by the hands of many of its past Forms, on battlefield, as also in the sacred security of home. It sees itself under the personages of maidens, and of women, of young and old men, and of children. . . . It feels itself dying more than once in those Forms. It expires as a hero-Spirit, and is led by the pitying Walkyries from the bloody battlefield back to the abode of Bliss under the shining foliage of Walhalla. It heaves its last sigh in another Form, and is hurled on to the cold, hopeless plane of remorse. It closes its innocent eyes in its last sleep, as an infant, and is forthwith carried along by the beauteous Elves of Light into another body — the doomed generator of Pain and Suffering. In each case the mists of death are dispersed, and pass from the eyes of the Soul-Ego, no sooner does it cross the Black Abyss that separates the Kingdom of the Living from the Realm of the Dead. Thus "Death" becomes but a meaningless word for it, a vain sound. In every instance the beliefs of the Mortal take objective life and shape for the Immortal, as soon as it spans the Bridge. Then they begin to fade, and disappear. . . .

"What is my Past?" enquires the Soul-Ego of Urd, the eldest of the Norn sisters. "Why do I suffer?"

A long parchment is unrolled in her hand, and reveals a long series of mortal beings, in each of whom the Soul-Ego recognizes one of its dwellings. When it comes to the last but one, [Clovis I, who slew the prophetess] it sees a blood-stained hand doing endless deeds of cruelty and treachery, and it shudders. . . . . . . Guileless victims arise around it, and cry to Orlog for vengeance.

"What is my immediate Present?" asks the dismayed Soul of Werdandi, the second sister.

"The decree of Orlog is on thyself!" is the answer. "But Orlog does not pronounce them blindly, as foolish mortals have it."

"What is my Future?" asks despairingly of Skuld, the third Norn sister, the Soul-Ego. "Is it to be for ever dark with tears, and bereaved of Hope?" . . .

No answer is received. But the Dreamer feels whirled through space, and suddenly the scene changes. The Soul-Ego finds itself on a, to it, long familiar spot, the royal bower, and the seat opposite the broken palm-tree. Before it stretches, as formerly, the vast blue expanse of waters, glassing the rocks and cliffs; there, too, is the lonely palm, doomed to quick disappearance. The soft mellow voice of the incessant ripple of the light waves now assumes human speech, and reminds the Soul-Ego of the vows formed more than once on that spot. And the Dreamer repeats with enthusiasm the words pronounced before.

"Never, oh, never shall I, henceforth, sacrifice vainglorious fame or ambition a single son of my motherland! Our world is so full of unavoidable misery, so poor with joys and bliss, and shall I add to its cup of bitterness the fathomless ocean of woe and blood, called WAR? Avaunt, such thought! . . . Oh, never more. . . ."

XI

Strange sight and change. . . . The broken palm which stands before the mental sight of the Soul-Ego suddenly lifts up its drooping trunk and becomes erect and verdant as before. Still greater bliss, the Soul-Ego finds himself as strong and as healthy as he ever was. In a stentorian voice he sings to the four winds a loud and a joyous song. He feels a wave of joy and bliss in him, and seems to know why he is happy.

He is suddenly transported into what looks a fairy-like Hall, lit with most glowing lights and built of materials, the like of which he had never seen before. He perceives the heirs and descendants of all the monarchs of the globe gathered in that Hall in one happy family. They wear no longer the insignia of royalty, but, as he seems to know, those who are the reigning Princes, reign by virtue of their personal merits. It is the greatness of heart, the nobility of character, their superior qualities of observation, wisdom, love of Truth and Justice, that have raised them to the dignity of heirs to the Thrones, of Kings and Queens. The crowns, by authority and the grace of God, have been thrown off, and they now rule by "the grace of divine humanity," chosen unanimously by recognition of their fitness to rule, and the reverential love of their voluntary subjects.

All around seems strangely changed. Ambition, grasping greediness or envy — miscalled Patriotism — exist no longer. Cruel selfishness has made room for just altruism and cold indifference to the wants of the millions no longer finds favour in the sight of the favoured few. Useless luxury, sham pretences — social and religious — all has disappeared. No more wars are possible, for the armies are abolished. Soldiers have turned into diligent, hard-working tillers of the ground, and the whole globe echoes his song in rapturous joy.

Kingdoms and countries around him live like brothers. The great, the glorious hour has come at last! That which he hardly dared to hope and think about in the stillness of his long, suffering nights, is now realized. The great curse is taken off, and the world stands absolved and redeemed in its regeneration! . . .

Trembling with rapturous feelings, his heart overflowing with love and philanthropy, he rises to pour out a fiery speech that would become historic, when suddenly he finds his body gone, or, rather, it is replaced by another body . . . Yes, it is no longer the tall, noble Form with which he is familiar, but the body of somebody else, of whom he as yet knows nothing. . . . Something dark comes between him and a great dazzling light, and he sees the shadow of the face of a gigantic timepiece on the ethereal waves. On its ominous dial he reads:

"NEW ERA: 970,995 YEARS SINCE THE INSTANTANEOUS DESTRUCTION BY PNEUMO-DYNO-VRIL OF THE LAST 2,000,000 OF SOLDIERS IN THE FIELD, ON THE WESTERN PORTION OF THE GLOBE. 971,000 SOLAR YEARS SINCE THE SUBMERSION OF THE EUROPEAN CONTINENTS AND ISLES. SUCH ARE THE DECREE OF ORLOG AND THE ANSWER OF SKULD . . . "

This glimpse into the distance future will be familiar to students of H. P. Blavatsky's great work The Secret Doctrine, and they will not be surprised at the prediction of the Norns that the end of war is still very far away. As for the efforts now being made to avert further wars by means of peace conferences, agreements to limit armaments, etc., President Hoover, in a speech on the problem of economic recovery in 1931, pointed out that "the world expenditure on all arms is now nearly five billions of dollars yearly, an increase of about seventy per cent over that previous to the Great War. We stand today with nearly 5,000,000 men actively under arms (i.e., in Europe and America) and 20,000,000 more in reserves. [*These vast forces, greatly exceeding those of the pre-war period, still are to be demobilized. even though twelves years have passed since the Armistice was signed, because of fear and of inability of nations to co-operate in mutual reductions. — Editor*]

He makes a strong effort and — is himself again. Prompted by the Soul-Ego to REMEMBER and ACT in conformity, he lifts his arms to Heaven and swears in the face of all nature to preserve peace to the end of his days — in his own country, at least.

-oOo-

A distant beating of drums and long cries of what he fancies in his dream are the rapturous thanksgivings, for the pledge just taken. An abrupt shock, loud clatter, and, as the eyes open, the Soul-Ego looks out through them in amazement. The heavy gaze meets the respectful and solemn face of the physician offering the usual draught. The train stops. He rises from his couch weaker and wearier than ever, to see around him endless lines of troops armed with a new and yet more murderous weapon of destruction — ready for the battlefield.

SANJNA
[Sanskrit for "Spiritual consciousness"]

www.ingramcontent.com/pod-product-compliance
Lightning Source LLC
LaVergne TN
LVHW041502070426
835507LV00009B/760